Arrowhawk

Arrowhawk

Lola M. Schaefer

ILLUSTRATED BY Gabi Swiatkowska

HENRY HOLT AND COMPANY   NEW YORK

*H*awk, young and strong, soared high above an open field. His large eyes searched the dried grasses below. A mouse raced in and out of the stubble. Hawk swooped down, snatched his prey, and carried it to a fence post. There in the autumn sun he tore and ate the mouse with his hooked beak.

TWWANGGGG! Out of nowhere, an arrow streaked through the air and pierced Hawk's upper thigh and tail. He screeched in pain. A flash of movement on his left signaled more danger. Stunned by the arrow, Hawk hesitated. Then he beat his wings, rose above his attacker, and flew into the distant trees.

Hawk tried to perch, but the arrow snagged on small branches. He flew higher until he landed on an open limb in a red oak. Pain pulsed through his body. He pecked wildly at the arrow lodged in his thigh, then he twisted his head and tried to push the arrow out of his tail. Blood seeped from the wounds, but the arrow did not budge. It was now a part of him.

For two days and nights Hawk rested high in the red oak.
He only left his roost to scoop water from a nearby stream.
Ignoring his pain, he cleaned his wounds by gently picking the
dirt and bugs from the openings. He then preened himself by sliding
his beak down the shaft of each feather and tucking it into place. Weary,
he slept.

By the third morning Hawk was hungry. He spotted a black rat snake in
the underbrush. He flapped his wings and glided down. SNATCH! Hawk
flew into a tree and held the snake against the limb. But when he bent
down to eat, his beak kept bumping into the arrow. After three tries Hawk
finally pushed his head far enough to the side so he could eat his prey.

During the next four weeks Hawk's wounds healed around the arrow, and he grew stronger. Then the days began to shorten and cooler winds blew from the north. Hawk's instinct to fly south led him away from the land he knew. He glided over harvested fields and busy barnyards. He sailed south over highways and rest areas. Sometimes he perched on poles or power lines, watching for unsuspecting prey.

Late one afternoon Hawk caught a mouse in a hayfield and carried it into a cottonwood tree. As he tried to land, the arrow wedged itself between the trunk and a branch. Hawk's right foot twisted backward. He could not move out of the tree.

Hawk flapped his wings several times, but he was still stuck. He pecked and jabbed and pulled the arrow with his beak. Nothing! Then, gathering all his remaining strength, he beat his wings and pushed with his feet. CRACK! Hawk's lower right leg snapped. At the same time, the arrow bent and the tip broke off. Pain shot through Hawk, but the push had been enough. He was free.

Hawk flew up to the top of the cottonwood. Not only had he broken his leg, but he had reopened the arrow wounds. Fresh blood trickled down his body. He was exhausted . . . and hungry. He had dropped the mouse and was too weak to hunt again. Before the sun set, Hawk was asleep.

Hawk awoke to cooler winds and pelting rains. His broken bone had not punctured the skin, but the leg was painful under his weight. Hawk winced every time he moved, so he only used his left leg to land and perch. For the next two days he took shelter in a grove of white pines and gradually the bone began to mend.

On the third morning Hawk flew out into the gray sky. Even though the arrow continued to weaken him, he traveled south for five miles before he stopped. He searched for a remote tree to perch, but all he saw were buildings, cars, and people.

Hawk rested on a telephone pole. From his lookout he spotted a field. Near dusk he circled the open area and found it teeming with mice, which were easily caught. Later he settled into a tall oak in a woods on the other side of the field. But every flight, every landing seemed to tire him more. Hawk closed his eyelids and slept.

Cold rains blanketed the area for the next five days. Chilled and hurting, Hawk remained in his safe roost. Finally one afternoon the sun broke through the trees. Still weak from the arrow, but hungry, Hawk left his perch. He was gliding over the field, now full of standing water, when he heard the chirping of birds close to the highway.

Hawk flew ahead and saw a covey of sparrows near the ground. They fluttered and bumped, one on top of another. If Hawk could capture a bird, it would be his first meal in days. On silent wings he dove, talons ready. Just as he reached for his prey, invisible net loops entangled his feet.

Hawk screeched loudly again and again. He couldn't reach the sparrows, and he couldn't fly away. Hawk beat his wings faster and faster. The more he struggled, the more his talons and feet became twisted in the snare. He fought, he screeched, he pecked, he flapped and flapped and flapped, until . . .

. . . darkness surrounded him. The fight was over. Every muscle relaxed as Hawk's head was covered and he was taken away in a warm box. Later, gloved hands held him high and he again beat his wings, struggling for freedom. But a firm grasp carried Hawk inside a building where an anesthetic helped him slip into sleep.

When he awoke the arrow was gone and his wounds were bandaged. Hawk sat in a small cage facing the woods. Weak and sore, he perched motionless, watching songbirds dart in the distance. Later a tray of food and a bowl of fresh water were set within his reach. Hawk ate and drank. Day by day he grew stronger.

After his wounds healed Hawk joined other hawks in a large flight cage. He had his own perch. He could flap his wings and glide from one end to the other. Between flights he preened. Many of his feathers felt longer and fuller. With the arrow gone, Hawk could now stretch and groom his tail feathers.

Every other day Hawk rode in a box to an open field. He wore leather straps that were attached to a flight line. Gloved hands tossed him into the air. Hawk felt the cold rush beneath him. He rose, flapped, and glided toward a small stand of trees. He knew this feeling of freedom well. But his flight always ended when the line ran out and pulled him back. Every time Hawk crossed that field, his muscles grew stronger and he flew faster than before.

Early one cold morning Hawk rode farther to another field, a field he knew. Gloved hands brought him into the sunlight. Again Hawk was held high. His leather straps were cut and fell to the ground. Hawk felt the north wind brush his face, and he heard a voice: "You survived, Arrowhawk. Fly home."

Familiar hands tossed him gently into the winter air. Hawk flapped his wings and skimmed the earth. Then he beat his wings harder, rose, and flew over the trees. And straight as an arrow, Hawk soared into the wild.

*T*he story of Arrowhawk is based on real events. A red-tailed hawk, less than a year old, survived a poacher's arrow for eight weeks in the wild. Through the combined efforts of concerned citizens, the media, and a raptor biologist (a person educated and trained to treat injured birds of prey), the young hawk's migratory course was charted. When several reports placed Arrowhawk at the same location for five days, a rescue was planned. The raptor biologist contacted a local falconer, who set a live trap, using sparrows as the bait. Arrowhawk was safely captured in late October and taken to a raptor center where licensed staff x-rayed him, performed surgery, treated his arrow wounds, and administered antibiotics to rid his body of infection. The hawk received further medical attention for six weeks. During that time his damaged feathers were removed and new ones were implanted with care and precision. Through regular exercise and carefully monitored test flights, the hawk's strength was restored. On December 24 Arrowhawk was taken back to the area where he was rescued. With a new set of tail feathers, strong muscles, and a healthy body, Arrowhawk was released into the wild.

Red-tailed hawks are among the most common raptors, birds of prey, found in North America. Their ideal habitat is a tall wooded area near an open field with a source of fresh water. Red-tailed hawks have the three identifying features of all birds of prey: large eyes, sharp talons, and a hooked beak. They hunt for live prey such as mice, rabbits, snakes, and birds by soaring over fields or watching from high perches. Red-tailed hawks help keep the number of rodents in check. Since an average hawk eats ten to twelve mice in one day, it can eat more than four thousand mice in a year.

Other birds of prey are owls, eagles, falcons, and osprey. Even though raptors have graced the skies for millions of years, in the last century our developing world has threatened their safety and future. Most raptors are injured or killed along highways. People throw trash by the side of the road, which attracts rodents. Birds of prey swoop down for their live food and are struck by trucks and automobiles. Still more birds suffer and die after eating poisonous chemicals intended to kill other animals or insects. And even though it is illegal, poachers claim the lives of many raptors each year with their senseless shooting.

But in the last twenty years we have gained a new understanding and respect for the role raptors play in the balance of nature. Strong protective laws have been written and enforced. The use of damaging chemicals has been greatly reduced. Reintroduction programs, such as those with peregrine falcons and eagles, have increased the populations of nearly extinct species. Still, that is not enough; we must educate our future citizens to guarantee that these mistakes will not be repeated. Conservation officials and raptor biologists are doing just that. These licensed and trained professionals visit schools and youth clubs with live presentations. Children see firsthand the majesty and dignity of these birds. They learn the importance of natural habitat, protective legislation, and land management. With our help, raptors will soar, dive, hunt, and grow for many more years.

For Adam
—L. M. S.

To my nephew Michel
—G. S.

A special thank-you to Janie,
who gave Arrowhawk his name and freedom.
—L. M. S.

Henry Holt and Company, LLC
Publishers since 1866
115 West 18th Street, New York, New York 10011
www.henryholt.com

Henry Holt is a registered trademark of Henry Holt and Company, LLC
Text copyright © 2004 by Lola M. Schaefer
Illustrations copyright © 2004 by Gabi Swiatkowska
Photograph of Arrowhawk © Steve Benson, used by permission
Designed by Donna Mark / Hand lettering by David Gatti
All rights reserved.
Distributed in Canada by H. B. Fenn and Company Ltd.

Library of Congress Cataloging-in-Publication Data
Schaefer, Lola M. Arrowhawk / Lola M. Schaefer ; illustrated by Gabi Swiatkowska.
Summary: Based on the true story of a bird of prey's survival after being struck by a
poacher's arrow. 1. Hawks—Juvenile fiction. [1. Hawks—Fiction. 2. Poaching—Fiction.
3. Wildlife rescue—Fiction.] I. Swiatkowska, Gabriela, ill. II. Title.
PZ10.3.S29Ar 2004   [Fic]—dc21   2003002528

ISBN 0-8050-6371-4 / First Edition—2004
Printed in the United States of America on acid-free paper.
1 3 5 7 9 10 8 6 4 2

The artist used acrylic on cold-pressed paper
to create the illustrations for this book.